To Wonder

by Hari Kleia

Illustrated by the Author

Order this book online at www.trafford.com
or email orders@trafford.com

Most Trafford titles are also available at major online book retailers.

Printed in the United States of America.

ISBN: 978-1-4669-6471-6 (sc)
978-1-4669-6470-9 (e)

Trafford rev. 10/19/2012

Trafford
PUBLISHING® www.trafford.com

North America & international

toll-free: 1 888 232 4444 (USA & Canada)

phone: 250 383 6864 ♦ fax: 812 355 4082

Remembering my younger brother

Miltiadis

For all the fun we had when we were children

And for how much we loved to wonder

I was thankful since I was a child

Thankful he was my brother

To Wonder

If we have a million and a billion

and a trillion things to tell

how to choose what to tell makes it

a million a billion and a trillion times hard

So let begin at the beginning as they tell

The first thing we know is that

the beginning was a long, long

long time ago

And we measure that time today

in millions and billions light years away

And let me try to say what one light year is

One light year tells that

light from one point in the sky

took one year to reach us here on earth

Now we know light from our sun

takes eight minutes to reach our planet

Just eight minutes

compared to one light year

is really no time at all

And if we consider that light has traveled

from as far as fourteen billion years away

that takes us now back

to where it all once began

Fourteen billion years back

they tell that nothing existed

not a single sun

not a star in the sky

No heavens and no earth

nothing at all

So how it all began?

Some tell:

At the beginning it was dark

and there was only God

And he was alone

and he was lonely

So one day God decided

from one to become many

And he said: Let there be light

And there was light

And in the light he created

the whole world

and you and me and all

and he was no longer alone

Some tell:

Once upon a time there was

one single point in an empty sky

And that single thing

that point in the sky

one day exploded

and there was light

They call that the "Big Bang"

And the Big Bang created all

in the skies above

the stars then the galaxies came alone

Then the heavens grew larger and larger

and our universe has today

its fourteen billion year old birthday

And is getting older day by day

and no one knows how old

it would be the last day

But still no one can truly tell

how it all once began

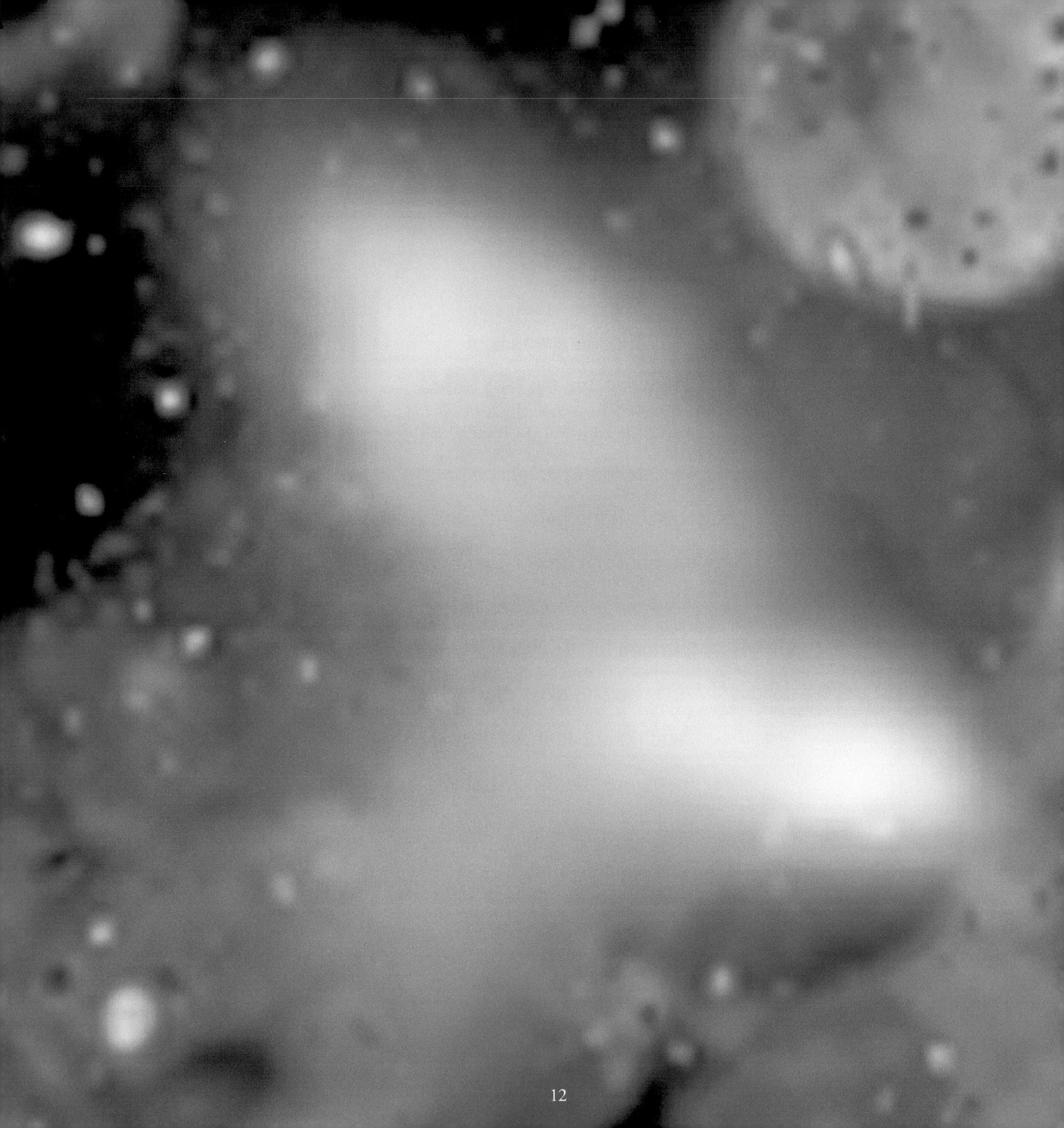

How old everything is

or how old the heaven is

Stars they tell were born in star nurseries

After stars were born

planets and moons came along

Our sun is a star

it was born not yesterday

but five billion years away

Earth one of the eight planets is

the only one we know where life exists

Earth was born in a similar way

four and a half billion years away

From stone, upon stone, upon stone

too many to count and too long

All coming together

by a force that attracted them all

the force of gravity they call

At the beginning there was fire

and fire alone was

for billions of years

melting stone upon stone

Then the water came along

Yet no one can tell how

if from comets in the form of ice it came

or up from the sky

in the form of rain it fell

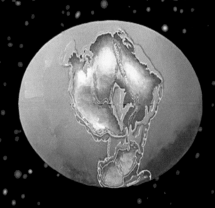

or even from underground

deep under the planet's ground

Water covered once they tell

most of the planet's ground

and from water they tell life began

First only one land, one continent

above the water did rise

They call that continent Pangaea

And that was many million years back

Then from earth's fiery ground

the one continent became two

then three, then four, five and six

and today seven continents

And if we count the islands

is far beyond count

Some tell from the water life came

Some tell from a planet faraway

And there are too many stories

of how it all began

The most important thing of all is that

now we are all on this planet's ground

And with you and me and all

are millions and billions

and trillions of creatures on this globe

Last of all the creatures we came along

and we wanted to know it all

They tell we were born just yesterday

yet we like to know it all

from day one to the last day

Yes we wonder more and more

of how it all came along

And we wonder more than

all the creatures on this globe

We wonder if life exists

somewhere else far away

We wonder if God exists or not

And if God exists

we would like to know where he is

and we all have plenty to ask him

But since God will tell not

we'll always wonder

And wondering we learn more and more

We wonder and we wonder

as if we are made to wonder

And how can we wonder not

as it all seems to be a wonder

Yet some tell that nothing is true

it is all an illusion

And it gets still harder for us

to reach a conclusion

But who really wants to reach a conclusion?

To wonder is good and I like to wonder

I think that even God

wonders with us

After all we are a wonder too

God's greatest wonder

or simply said

a wondering wonder!

Looking through a telescope today

we can see the universe

farther than ever before

We see new stars born

near and far away

we just can't count how many

We see how galaxies move

away from each other

And they move faster and faster

Faster than we can count

They tell that

in billions of years from now

all galaxies in the sky

will move so far apart

they'll empty the sky

Maybe then

like at the beginning as they tell

it will be once again

one single point in the sky

Now if this story ends

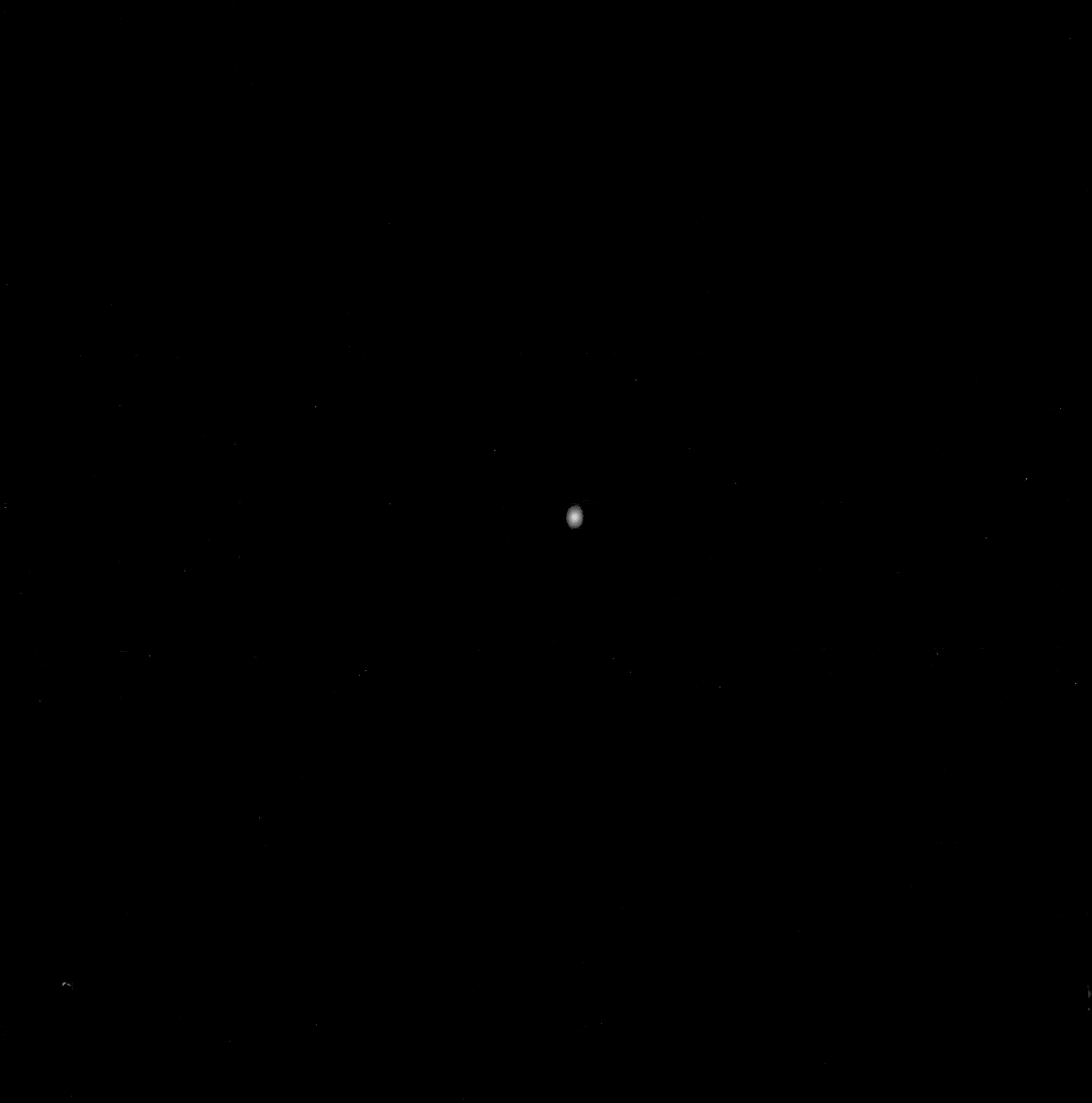

the same way it once began

let us think of the first story

The first story tells that

At the beginning it was dark

and there was only God

And God was alone

and he was lonely

And from one decided

to become many

They also tell that at the end

God will from many become one

once again

And in our story once again

the beginning reminds the end

Remember

God from one became a world

and

One point became a heaven

And I wonder now again

What if at the beginning

God and the point was the same

What if God and the point was one?

And the point was God!

And God was the point.

Printed in the United States
by Baker & Taylor Publisher Services